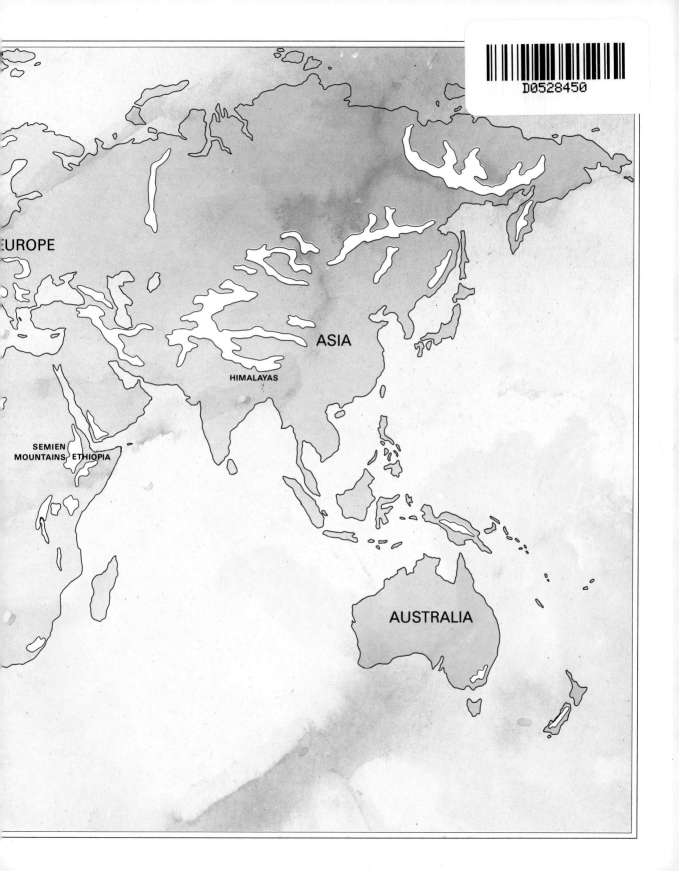

EUROPE

ASIA

HIMALAYAS

SEMIEN
MOUNTAINS ETHIOPIA

AUSTRALIA

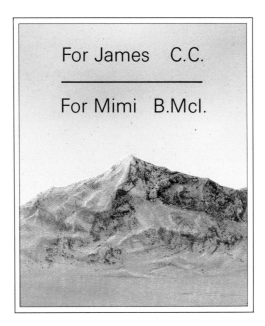

For James   C.C.

For Mimi   B.Mcl.

'The marmots' winter burrow'
and labelled flowers
illustrated by David Wright

First published 1984 by
Walker Books Ltd,
17-19 Hanway House, Hanway Place,
London W1P 9DL

Printed and bound in Spain
by Artes Graficas Toledo, S.A.
DL-TO-164-84

British Library Cataloguing in Publication Data
Catchpole, Clive
Mountains. – (The Living World)
1. Mountain ecology – Juvenile literature
I. Title   II. McIntyre, Brian   III. Series
574.5'264   QH541.5.1765

ISBN 0-7445-0059-1

THE LIVING WORLD
MOUNTAINS

By Dr CLIVE CATCHPOLE
Illustrated by BRIAN McINTYRE

WALKER BOOKS
LONDON

The top of a high mountain is one of the most dangerous places on earth. Covered in ice and snow and lashed by fierce gales, nothing can survive there for long. Cold is the main enemy. The higher you go, the colder it becomes. The lower slopes are often thickly forested, and many mountain animals move down to shelter there in winter. Above the trees are alpine meadows, grazed in summer by animals such as the chamois. Higher still comes bare rock. Here only the hardiest animals can withstand the low temperatures and strong winds.

Edelweiss

Spring gentian

Cushion pink

The plants which grow above the tree-line are tough and hardy. They must tolerate very low temperatures, strong winds and sparse, rocky soil. Yet in the European Alps, some of the most beautiful flowers in the world grow between 2,000 and 3,000 metres. Small, compact, and hugging the rocky surface, alpine plants have long roots to anchor and search deep for unfrozen water. Many lie dormant throughout the colder months. Some alpine flowers, such as the snowy-white edelweiss, have a hairy covering that holds in warmth and moisture.

Mouse-ear chickweed

Alpine cinquefoil

Alpine aster

Wherever there are flowers there are insects which pollinate them. Grasshoppers, beetles and butterflies are all found high above the tree-line. Some of these cold-blooded animals can survive because they have a special chemical in their blood which acts as an anti-freeze. Many mountain insects are wingless, or fly very little, as flying in strong winds is difficult and dangerous. But in a sudden period of calm, the Himalayan air can fill with thousands of Apollo butterflies. Some are found at over 5,000 metres, where they lay their eggs on the icy rocks.

The ptarmigan is a bird which is specially adapted to living and breeding high in the mountains. In summer its mottled plumage blends perfectly into the rocky hills, protecting it from birds of prey like falcons. Ptarmigan are vegetarian, and particularly fond of heather shoots.

When snow covers the ground in winter, the ptarmigan keeps its camouflage by turning almost completely white. The new white feathers form a warm winter coat. The mountain hare also changes colour, but more gradually, as new white fur grows through its grey-brown summer coat.

In the high Andes of South America, several kinds of rodent manage to live and breed way above the tree-line. They survive the intense cold mainly because of their thick fur. The most remarkable of all is the chinchilla, which is found as high as 6,000 metres. Its fine blue-grey fur is one of the warmest and most beautiful coats in all nature. It is so dense that, unlike other mountain rodents, the chinchilla does not have to spend as much time sheltering in its burrow. The chinchilla even comes out to nibble plants in the freezing night air.

The Rocky Mountain goat of North America is probably the best equipped of all larger alpine animals. To counter the intense cold it has several insulating layers. Coarse, shaggy hair extends to the knees, and underneath this is a coat of short, thick wool. There is a very thick hide, and finally a layer of fat beneath the skin. These animals will eat almost anything, and their teeth can deal with the toughest vegetation. The Rocky Mountain goat is a superb climber. Its hoof has hard, sharp edges, and a special non-slip pad in the middle to tackle treacherous crags.

The largest grazing animals in the Andes are all members of the camel family. The sure-footed llama is the traditional beast of burden, whereas the alpaca is used mainly to provide wool and meat. Both these are domesticated animals, and may have originated from the truly wild forms – the guanaco and the vicuña. The elegant vicuña is the smallest, but can graze well above 4,000 metres where air is thin and hard to breathe. The famous soft, fine vicuña wool grows like a bib below the neck.

The Semien Mountains of Ethiopia are the home of a mountain-dwelling monkey, the gelada baboon. Geladas roam the arid, desert-like plateaux in vast herds. Each male has a harem of females which he defends against other males by frequent chases and fights. The shaggy, hairy coat offers some protection against the cold nights of the high Semien. There is also more shelter available in the gorges where the baboons spend the night. Geladas are extremely agile and can scamper up and down the rocky cliffs at amazing speeds.

The marmots' winter burrow

In summer, the meadows of the European Alps are grazed by the alpine marmot. Emerging from its burrow, the marmot often stands upright and peers round in search of its main enemy, the golden eagle. In winter, when the meadows are covered in snow, it is impossible to feed. But the marmots have grown fat in summer, and retire to their burrows to sleep the winter away in a state of hibernation. Their temperature drops and their heartbeat and breathing become very slow. Hibernating marmots can survive for many months on their store of body fat.

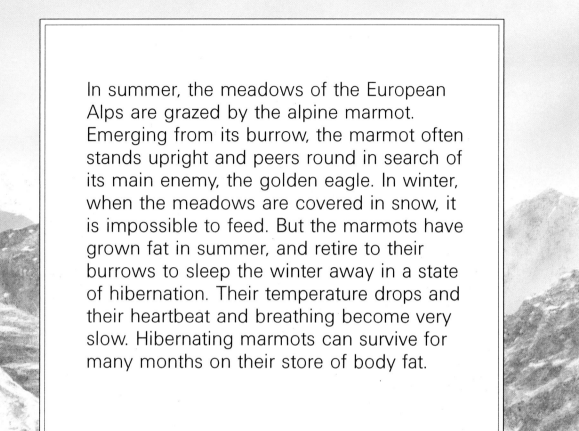

The most ferocious of large mountain animals is the grizzly bear, found mainly on wooded slopes of mountains in Alaska and Canada. Like marmots, grizzlies ride out the worst of winter by hibernating in a den, often buried deep under snow. But theirs is not a true hibernation, and in mild weather they may wake up. In spring they emerge to eat roots, squirrels, chipmunks, and even salmon scooped from icy rivers. The female gives birth to her cubs in the den, and is very protective towards them, charging any hunter foolish enough to come too close.

The mountain lion is found in many parts of the New World. It is called the puma in South America, but is known as the cougar in North America. The cougar often hunts well above the tree-line, even in snowy conditions. It likes to stalk its prey before making a sudden dash, or it may wait in ambush on an overhanging rock. One of its main sources of food is bighorn sheep. The bighorns are agile enough on the mountains, but no match for the powerful cat, which may weigh over 100 kilograms when it is fully grown.

The Andean condor is a giant among birds and one which, through flight, has truly mastered the mountain world. Weighing over 12 kilograms and with a wing-span of about three metres, it is a majestic sight soaring high among the peaks. With wings outstretched, a condor can soar effortlessly for over 100 kilometres at a time. It is constantly on the lookout, for the great bird is also a scavenger, a kind of vulture. The condor searches for signs of dead or dying animals, those who have succumbed at last to the harsh world of the high mountains.

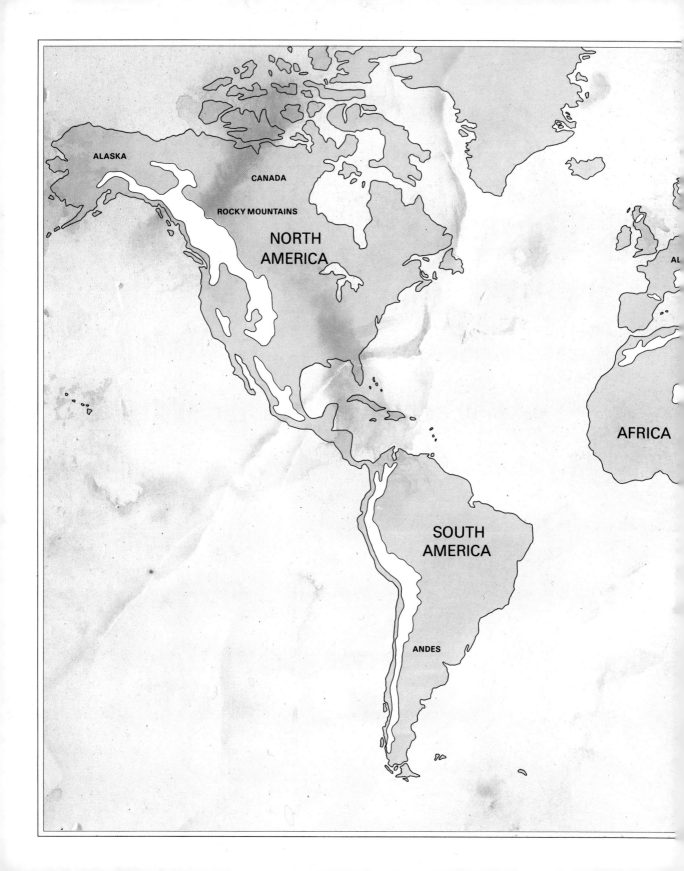